Connell Short Guide
to
Ian McEwan's

_____

Atonement

_____

by
Theo Tait

Contents

Introduction

When *Atonement* was published in 2001, Ian McEwan was already one of Britain's leading novelists, but his new book took his career to a different level. John Updike noted that whereas McEwan's previous novels had tended to be "short, smart and dark", *Atonement* was "a beautiful and majestic fictional panorama". His earlier fiction had consisted of two identifiable cycles. First came two short story collections and two short novels, *The Cement Garden* (1979) and *The Comfort of Strangers* (1981), which earned him the nickname "Ian Macabre". These works combine lurid detail – sexual aberration, violence, cruelty – with a steely detachment; his prose was often described as "surgical". After that followed a series of five slightly longer novels which retain a nightmarish edge: they feature fatal balloon accidents; hideous protracted murders; dogs trained by the Gestapo to rape. However, they also have an explicit political or social aspect. *The Child in Time* (1987) begins with a child-snatching, but widens out into an examination of child-rearing and Thatcherism. *The Innocent* (1990) and *Black Dogs* (1992) both examine 20th century European history against fraught personal relationships, while *Enduring Love* (1992) turns a story of sexual obsession into a wider argument about rationality and irrationality, evolution and self-interest.

Atonement preserves some of these features. At its centre is a shocking episode, or two shocking episodes, concerning taboo sexual desire; and this private drama is played out against a larger historical canvas. It has the tough-minded precision of his earlier work, but seems to take place in a different key – grander, more expansive and warmer. It is sophisticated and features a range of styles set over four different periods of time, yet in some ways it resembles a mainstream family saga, a conventional love story.

Atonement was very well received both by the critics and by the public. James Wood described it as "certainly" McEwan's "finest and most complex novel". Frank Kermode agreed, calling it "easily his finest", while Hermione Lee suggested it was his best yet – though some critics, like many readers since, complained about the frustrating ending. His previous novel, *Enduring Love*, had been a bestseller, but *Atonement* was a much bigger commercial success, selling more than four million copies in Britain and abroad during its first decade in print, and spawning a successful film. Along with the novels that followed it, *Saturday* (2005) and *On Chesil Beach* (2007), it helped establish McEwan as, in The New Yorker's words, "England's national novelist".

Designed to be read on several levels at once, *Atonement* is both a gripping yarn about love, survival and lives turned upside down, and also a reflection on truth and memory, guilt and atonement, experience and literary tradition.

A summary of the plot

Part One takes place over the course of a day and a night, during a heat wave in the summer of 1935, at the Tallis family's grand country house in Surrey. Briony Tallis, 13, a budding writer, is preparing to stage a melodrama that she has written in order to impress her brother Leon, who is coming home that evening with his friend, a confectionary tycoon named Paul Marshall. She dragoons her visiting cousins – Lola de Quincey, 15 and twins Jackson and Pierrot, 9, "refugees from a bitter domestic civil war"– into taking part.

Briony's mother, Emily, who suffers from migraines, spends much of her time in bed, while her father, a senior civil servant, is a distant presence, away in London. Her sister, Cecilia, has recently graduated from Cambridge, and has been sent out by her mother to collect wildflowers for Paul Marshall's bedroom. She takes a valuable vase, given to her Uncle Clem shortly before his death in the First World War, to fill it in the fountain at the front of the house. There she encounters her "childhood friend and university acquaintance", Robbie Turner – the son of the Tallises' charlady and protégé of her father Jack – who is working in the garden. Their relationship has been "difficult" since Cambridge, where Robbie was sent at Cecilia's father's expense, and they argue, over his plan to train as a doctor, again bankrolled by her father. Robbie offers to fill the vase for her. She refuses; he tries to grab the vase and breaks it; a section of the lip falls into the water. Furious, Cecilia strips down to her underwear, and dives into the fountain to retrieve it.

Briony, looking out of the nursery window, misinterprets the scene: she thinks that Robbie has ordered Cecilia to take her clothes off and dive in. Cecilia tries to repair the vase, and Leon and Paul Marshall arrive. Cecilia learns, to her annoyance, that Leon has invited Robbie to dinner. At his mother's bungalow, Robbie writes a letter to Cecilia, attempting to explain himself. In a roundabout way, it suggests that he loves her, but he spoils it with an obscene declaration of his infatuation. He then writes a fair copy. Walking over towards the big house, he meets Briony and asks her to take the letter to Cecilia. Only when Briony is in the house does he realise that he has given her the obscene version. Cecilia receives the letter on the terrace, and thinks: "Of course, of course." She also realises that Briony must have opened it.

Soon afterwards, Briony goes into the library, and sees Robbie and Cecilia having sex; she thinks that he is attacking her sister, and that he is a dangerous "maniac". A tense, hot dinner follows, during which it emerges that the twins have run away. The dinner guests go out into the grounds to look for them. Briony stumbles upon Lola being raped by a man who then disappears into the dark. Lola can't or won't say who it was; Briony thinks, or decides, that it was Robbie.

The police arrive; Briony is interrogated and gives a statement blaming Robbie. She also finds Robbie's letter to Cecilia, and shows it to her brother and the police. Cecilia is very angry. At dawn, Robbie re-emerges with the twins, whom he has found. He is arrested and driven away by the police. His mother screams at the car as it passes.

Part Two is set in France in 1940. Robbie, having been convicted of rape, imprisoned, and then drafted into the army, is retreating across the countryside towards Dunkirk ahead of the advancing German forces. He is wounded, with shrapnel in his side. He is with two corporals, Nettle and Mace. They stay the night in a French family's barn.

That night, Robbie remembers his last meeting with Cecilia, in 1939, shortly after his release from prison. They have remained dedicated to each other, writing each other letters every week during his time in prison. Cecilia has cut off all contact with her family since 1935, and has trained as a nurse. Lately, Robbie has learnt that Briony thinks she was wrong to blame him for Lola's rape, and wants to change her evidence.

The next day the three men join a long line of retreating soldiers, civilians and vehicles on the road to Dunkirk. An officer tries to recruit them for a small counter-attack, but the corporals bluff their way out of it. They are strafed and bombed by German planes. They finally reach the sea at Bray Dunes. Robbie is feeling increasingly light-headed; his wound is throbbing. The scene on the beach is chaotic. In the resort of Bray, there are soldiers drinking in ruined cafes. In one, angry soldiers have surrounded an RAF man, whom they blame for not protecting them from the Luftwaffe. The corporals and Turner rescue him. Having lost Mace, Robbie and Nettle are given food and drink by a Frenchwoman. They find shelter in a bombed-out basement; Robbie eats and falls into a delirious sleep.

Part Three takes place in London in 1940. Briony is a probationary nurse at St Thomas's Hospital; her training is described in some detail. She is also writing stories, and has submitted one to the literary magazine Horizon. Briony receives a letter from her father, telling her that Paul Marshall and Lola de Quincey are to be married, which she regards as a "confirmation" of her suspicion that Marshall was the rapist.

After a half-day off, she returns to the hospital to find that the casualties of Dunkirk – large numbers of badly wounded men – are arriving at the hospital. Briony cleans infected wounds, pulls out shrapnel, and talks to a young Frenchman who dies in her arms. Following a very long shift, she returns to her room and finds a letter from Cyril Connolly at Horizon rejecting her novella – which turns out to be a version of the events in Part One – but encouraging her and suggesting improvements. A few days later, Briony walks across London to Clapham to witness the marriage of Paul Marshall and Lola. She then walks further south to Balham, and finds Cecilia living in a down-at-heel terrace. Cecilia is furious with her. Robbie, who unexpectedly emerges from the bedroom, is angrier still. Briony is relieved that he is still alive. The couple insist that Briony should go to her parents and inform them that her evidence was false. They are still under the impression that the rapist was Danny Hardman, a servant at the house; she reveals to them that it was Paul Marshall. Briony apologises to the pair and resolves to make her atonement. Part Three is signed, at the end, "BT, London 1999".

The epilogue is set in London in 1999. It is Briony's 77th birthday. She visits the Imperial War Museum, shortly after finishing the novel that constitutes the rest of the book. She has just learnt that she is suffering from vascular dementia, which will eventually rob her of her speech and sanity. As her taxi arrives, she sees, by chance, Paul and Lola, now Lord and Lady Marshall, who are benefactors of the museum.

She returns home, and then sets off in the afternoon in another taxi for the Tallis family house, now Tilney's Hotel, for her birthday party – organised by Pierrot's grandson Charles. The family assembles in the old library: mostly the children, grandchildren and great-grandchildren of Pierrot, Jackson (now dead), and Leon (now confined to a wheelchair). Writing at her desk in the early morning, Briony reveals that the current book has gone through half a dozen drafts, between January 1940 and March 1999; she has been unable to publish it before the Marshalls' death, for fear of being sued for libel. All her previous drafts, she says, were "pitiless"; it is only in the final version that "my lovers end well". Briony then suggests strongly that Robbie died of septicaemia at Bray Dunes in 1940, and that Cecilia was killed later that year by the bomb in Balham; that she never saw either of them again.

What kind of novel is *Atonement*?

In Chapter Four, Briony approaches her sister

Cecilia, on the verge of tears about her play, The Trials of Arabella. "The whole thing's a mistake," she says. "It's the wrong genre!" *Atonement* is a self-conscious work, marinated in the history of the English novel, which is itself also a meditation on literary form: on the need to find the right genre for expression. The book occupies no very obvious genre, or perhaps more accurately, several at once. It could be called a postmodernist novel – a term for fiction which pastiches or imitates other, earlier styles, and which does so in a self-conscious and knowing way.

The first part of the novel, for instance, is a pastiche of a country house novel, a tradition in English literature that stretches from Jane Austen via Henry James to Elizabeth Bowen – all writers alluded to in the text – and on to the present day. Specifically, the story echoes L.P. Hartley's *The Go-Between*, a 1953 novel set in the year 1900. McEwan himself has acknowledged the inspiration, saying that Hartley's book "in some way formed the seed for" *Atonement*. Both novels feature a child protagonist who stumbles across an adult love affair between two people of different social classes. In both cases, the child is employed to carry a letter between the lovers, with disastrous results. Both feature an epilogue in which a character looks back on the episode, many years later, after a world war. There are so many similarities between the two books, in fact, that some critics have seen

Atonement as a rewriting of *The Go-Between*.

However, if the seed for *Atonement* was provided by Hartley, the style and many of the incidents in the first half recall Virginia Woolf. Her novel *The Waves* (1931) is mentioned as an influence in Part Three. As in Woolf's *Mrs Dalloway* (1925), Part One is set over the course of one long day. The dinner party recalls the dinner party at the end of the first section of Woolf's *To The Lighthouse* (1927). In general, the book is so full of echoes of writers from the first half of the 20th century (see the section on allusions) that McEwan has been described by Geoff Dyer as "retrospectively inserting himself into the Pantheon of British novelists" of the period.

Atonement is also a coming-of-age story, and a love story of a fairly traditional kind – about ardent lovers kept apart by adverse circumstance – as well as a war story. And, of course, it is a historical novel. When Hartley wrote *The Go-Between*, he was remembering the world of his own childhood. For McEwan, however, born in 1948, the novel's setting had to be recreated from other books and sources: novels, archives, memoirs, poems, his father's memories. Furthermore, *Atonement* is a meta-fiction: a novel that tells the story of how it came to be told. By the end of Part Three it has been confirmed that Briony is the author of everything we have so far read; she is both a character and the narrator. This is called a recursive structure – a story within a story.

The novel as a whole could be compared to another postmodern work, *The French Lieutenant's Woman* (1969) by John Fowles. Like *Atonement*, Fowles's novel is a partial pastiche (in his case, of a Victorian novel) which offers alternative endings, including one traditionally happy one. It also features a narrator who intrudes into the story to discuss his decisions, responsibilities, and research processes.

How the story is told

The turning point

Most novels feature a crucial turning point. Coming-of-age stories often centre on the summer when everything changes; the "moment in childhood", as Graham Greene put it, "when the door opens and lets the future in". (Briony, in the vital fountain scene in Chapter Three, senses that she has suddenly been given "privileged access across the years to adult behaviour" (p.39).) In Ian McEwan novels, the turning point tends to take a particularly traumatic form. His characters often find themselves, like the narrator of *Enduring Love*, "running towards a catastrophe... a kind of furnace in whose heat identities and fates would buckle into new shapes". They find their ordered lives disrupted by horrific incidents – the snatching of a child, a freak accident, a murder – which forms the pivot for the story. As John Lanchester points out, McEwan novels often "begin in a nightmare, and then set out to explain the nightmare, to control and rationalise it". In *Atonement*, the pivot – the nightmare – is a pair of crimes: the rape of Lola, and Briony's subsequent false accusation. It is the central trauma which buckles all the characters' lives into new shapes; the whole book is designed to dramatise and examine the consequences of this moment. The trauma, as James Wood argues, "inaugurates a loss of innocence", an ejection from a happier world: in the case of Robbie and Cecilia, from the world of their childhood, the house and the park; in Briony's case, from a time when she was free of guilt.

McEwan novels tend to slow down in the moments before the catastrophe occurs: as the narrator of *Enduring Love* says in the celebrated first chapter of that book, "I'm lingering in the prior moment because it was a time when other outcomes were still possible". This technique allows McEwan to examine, minutely, the chain of causation that leads to the catastrophe; to see how things turned out as they did. Robbie, for instance, decides to search for the twins on his own. "This decision, as he was to acknowledge many times, transformed his life" (p.144). In *Atonement*, the pace is slowed right down, so that the build-up to

Saoirse Ronan as Briony and James McAvoy as Robbie in Joe Wright's film adaptation of Atonement

the trauma occupies most of the first half of the novel. The technique also ratchets up the suspense, a form of slow torture that readers enjoy despite themselves.

Prolepsis

Prolepsis or anticipation – announcing or hinting what will happen in the future – is crucial to McEwan's method. The strategy is used throughout *Atonement*, from the start of the first chapter to very near the end. When Briony reads her play to her mother, we are told that she "was hardly to know it then, but this was the project's highest point of fulfilment" (p.4). In the final scene featuring Robbie and Cecilia, their fate is prefigured by this sentence: "They stood outside Balham tube station, which in three months' time would achieve its terrible form of fame in the Blitz" (p.348). The book, while looking back to the events it describes, also looks forward to their consequences. Meanwhile, particularly in the first section, the plot often stops and starts; one scene overlaps with another. Past and future become mixed up: "All day long, [Cecilia] realised, she had been feeling strange, and seeing strangely, as though everything was already long in the past, made more vivid by posthumous ironies she could not quite grasp" (p.48). Even small details become proleptic: the Amo bar, which Paul Marshall describes in Part One, turns up in the soldiers' kit in Part Two.

Prolepsis is partly a device to keep the reader reading. McEwan has said that he aims "to incite a naked hunger" in his audience; he creates narrative tension by revealing some pieces of information, while simultaneously concealing others. There are a series of ominous announcements in *Atonement*. They start off quite vague. We are told that Briony had no secrets: "Nothing in her life was sufficiently interesting or shameful to merit hiding... None of this was particularly an affliction; or rather, it appeared so only in retrospect, once a solution had been found" (p.5). Later on they become more explicit: "Within the half hour Briony would commit her crime" (p.156).

But prolepsis is also appropriate to an account of events that took place in the 1930s but which is written, as we learn later in the novel, in the 1990s. "Six decades later," we are told, as Briony observes the scene at the fountain, "she would describe how at the age of thirteen she had written her way through a whole history of literature..." (p.41). This alerts us to the fact that the story is written with the benefit of hindsight; combining the point of view of a 13-year-old girl with that of an elderly woman. It prepares us for the novel's preoccupation with how memory reshapes reality. Briony goes on to think: "Now there was nothing left of the dumb show by the fountain beyond what survived in memory, in three separate and overlapping memories. The truth had become as ghostly as invention." Finally, as the critic John Mullan points out, the use of prolepsis "enacts" the characters' "loss of innocence" – their ejection from a happier, pastoral world. As Robbie walks over for dinner at the big house, we are told: "In years to come he would often think back to this time, when he walked along the footpath that made a shortcut through a corner of the oak woods" (p.144).

Point of view

As she watches the episode at the fountain, Briony realises that she "could write the scene three times over, from three points of view" (p.40). *Atonement* itself is written from a variety of point of views. It is narrated, with the exception of the first-person epilogue, in free indirect style, a form of third person narration which gives particular access to one character's thoughts. Part One rotates, chapter by chapter, through various different perspectives: first Briony's, then Cecilia's, then Briony's again, then their mother Emily's, then Briony's again, then Robbie's, and so on. Part Two is written from Robbie's point of view; Part Three from Briony's. This is an attempt to dramatise the "separate and overlapping memories" mentioned above, though the recursive structure complicates this – it is eventually revealed that each one is in fact Briony's approximation of their perspective, a perspective on a perspective.

Another insight of Briony's from the fountain scene is "how easy it was to get everything wrong, completely wrong" (p.39). Indeed she herself misunderstands the episode: she thinks that Robbie is "imperiously" ordering Cecilia into the water (p.38). The novel acts out these misinterpretations on a larger canvas. Cecilia misinterprets Robbie's awkwardness with her as being derived from class resentment, "for being in a different circle at Cambridge, for not having a charlady for a mother" (p.27). In fact, it is because he has fallen in love with her. Emily thinks that Paul Marshall "might not be such a bad sort, if he was prepared to pass the time of day entertaining children" (p.69), when in fact he is assaulting Lola. Briony thinks that Robbie is raping Cecilia when, we learn later, they are joyfully making love: "her immediate understanding was that she had interrupted an attack, a hand to hand fight" (p.123). Later, of course, Briony completely misinterprets the rape of Lola, with life-changing effects for the cast. Cecilia and Robbie will also misinterpret that crime, blaming it on Danny Hardman. Robbie thinks that Briony's girlish passion for him might have motivated her to blame him; we know that this is not so, since we are told that she "immediately forgot about it" (p.342).

The point of this is twofold. First, the novel insists that finding out "what really happened" (p.371) is very difficult; that people get things very wrong, and they reinterpret the world around them to fit their misapprehensions, sometimes with terrible consequences; the "weary, self-evident world" can in fact "be reinvented by a child" (p.68). The second is a more general one, to do, again, with truth and fantasy, memory and storytelling. Memory is a form of reinvention. Briony knows, when she tells stories about 1935, that it is "not the long-ago morning she was recalling so much as her subsequent accounts of it" (p.41). As McEwan wrote in the

introduction to his libretto *Or Shall We Die?* (1983),
"the observer is part of what he observes".

Style

Excluding the epilogue, *Atonement* divides into
two very different sections: a first half set in a
grand house in peacetime, which is slow-moving
and stately, though tense; and the wartime
sections, which are faster-moving, grimier, and
more matter-of-fact. McEwan told an interviewer
that he wrote Part One in "a slightly mannered
prose, slightly held in, a little formal, a tiny bit
archaic", with which he felt he could "evoke the
period best". The Dunkirk sections, however, are
written "in a choppier prose with shorter, simpler
sentences". "On the battlefield," he felt, "the
subordinate clause has no place."

In Part One, most sentences are long – the first
of the book lasts six lines. There are a great deal of
qualifying words, and complex figures of
comparison: "The cool high shade of the woods
was a relief, the sculpted intricacies of the tree
trunks enchanting" (p.18). The style might be
called pastoral, in that there are many images of
vegetation and water. The metaphors and similes
are often extravagant and overstated: Briony loses
herself in a "tempest of composition" (p.3); Cecilia
feels a "blossoming need for a cigarette"; the park
is "roasting like a savannah" and the long grass is
"already stalked by the leonine yellow of high

summer" (p.38). It is a prose that elevates and dramatises relatively minor perceptions, just as Briony longs for excitement. As Cyril Connolly's letter suggests, the style aims to examine "the crystalline present moment", to "delve into mysteries of perception", to "permit the vagaries and unpredictability of the private self to be explored" (p.312). See, for instance, the emphasis on Emily's migraine, producing "illuminated points in her vision, little pinpricks, as though the worn fabric of the visible world was being held up against a far brighter light" (p.63), or the visual close-up of Lola touching a suitcase: "The polished metal was cool, and her touch left little patches of shrinking condensation"(p.56). Martin Amis regards Part One as the greatest achievement of McEwan's career.

In Part Two and Part Three, you are far more likely to find simple, functional sentences, such as "They stopped so that he could consult the map" (p.191), or "On Saturday morning Briony left the hospital at eight without eating breakfast and walked with the river on her right, upstream" (p.318). McEwan relies more on action and detail to portray the characters' mental states; where the first part is heightened and concerned with subjective perception, the second half is vivid, unsentimental and objective. But this is not to say that it is dull or uncomplicated; rather it shows what James Wood calls a "disciplined richness of style". There are occasional flourishes, made more striking by the understated writing. Robbie, for instance, feels "the pain in his side like a flash of colour" (p.236), and the cloud from the burning fuel depots hangs over Dunkirk "like an angry father" (p.240). McEwan's prose is often described as "surgical"; in the hospital sections, it is quite literally so. It looks at places "intimate, and never intended to be seen" (p.302):

> *"She could see through his missing cheek to his upper and lower molars, and the tongue glistening, and hideously long." (p.301)*

Detail

Attention to detail is one of McEwan's hallmarks as a writer; he is famous for the lengths which he goes to research his subjects. He pays a great deal of attention to what Henry James called "solidity of specification": specifying the external details in such a way as to make the scene solid and convincing. McEwan will explain, for instance, that the island temple at the house was built "in the style of Nicholas Revett in the late 1780s" (p.72); or that the vase Cecilia was looking for was on not just a table, but "an American cherry-wood table" (p.20); or that an abandoned ambulance on the Dunkirk road was "a gift of the British residents of Brazil" (p.218). For most readers, these individual pieces of information will mean little on their own. But, as Briony says in the epilogue, "these little things, the pointillist approach to verisimilitude" cumulatively make a lot of difference; she compares novelists to "policemen in a search team", who "go on hands and knees and crawl our way towards to the truth" (p.359). Pointillism is a form of painting which involves building up a picture carefully by placing a profusion of dots on the canvas. If you get each individual dot right, then you will produce a convincing picture.

The Dunkirk section begins with the sentence: "There were horrors enough, but it was the unexpected detail that threw him and afterwards would not let him go" (p.191). Soon after this, Robbie sees a leg in a tree – "wedged in the first forking of the trunk, bare, severed cleanly above the knee" (p.192). McEwan has written that while composing *Atonement*, he was "particularly fascinated by the telling detail, or the visually rich episode that projected unspoken emotion". In this case, the presentation is entirely neutral, but the fact that the leg is "perfect... pale, smooth, small enough to be a child's" speaks volumes.

Throughout the book, and especially in Part Two, McEwan wrings powerful effects from telling, unexpected details. For instance, it is reasonably well known that Allied forces destroyed much of their equipment before they were evacuated, to stop it falling into German hands. But it is much less well known that the French cavalry shot their horses or that the British burned piles of bibles, for the same reason. That scene in the book, with the French officer walking along the line while the horses "patiently waited their turn", is a particularly piteous "enactment of defeat" (p.219). The novel's "psychological acuity", suggests Geoff Dyer, derives from its "fidelity to a precisely delineated reality".

Ultimately, though, the novel also takes us behind the details. We learn that in Briony's earlier draft of the first section it is a Ming vase, not a Meissen vase, which Robbie breaks; that in a draft of the Dunkirk section, she had written that a Stuka carries a "single thousand-ton bomb" and was later corrected by a retired colonel to "thousand-pound" (p.360). This is one of many ways that the book draws attention to its own artifice, to how it constructs its own reality. And this, in turn, can lead the reader to question all sorts of details. Does the whole history of the vase really make sense? Would it not, as the novel suggests, be "inconvenient... to fight a war with Meissen porcelain under one arm"? (p.23). Or to use such a valuable item to put flowers in? And aren't some of the carefully specified facts of the Tallises's world quite odd? Why is the cook preparing "perhaps a hundred potatoes" for their unseasonal roast? That's 12.5 per dinner guest.

Symbols and motifs

Perhaps the most obvious symbol in the novel is the vase broken in Chapter Two. It is, first off, an emblem of war and death – it was given to the children's uncle as a recognition of his bravery in World War One and "delivered to the Tallis home some months after Uncle Clem's burial" (p.23). It is fragile, and also extremely valuable. So it is fitting that Cecilia and Robbie find themselves struggling over it; Robbie's status, his lack of wealth, is a bone of contention between the two; their relationship will turn out to be easily destroyed.

The idea of the vase is picked up as a metaphor at various important moments. We learn that "the glazed surface" of Briony's conviction, concerning her accusation against Robbie, develops "blemishes and hairline cracks" in the week after his arrest (p.168). Two triangular pieces break off the lip of the vase; there's also a triangular piece missing from one of the twin's ears. Frank Kermode argues that the "premonitory damage echoes what happens to other fragile objects highly valued," including "life itself". From Briony's experience of tending the wounded of Dunkirk, she learns "a simple, obvious thing she had always known: that a person is, among all else, a material thing, easily torn, not easily mended" (p.304). A few pages later, we learn that Uncle Clem's vase has been dropped and smashed.

TEN FACTS ABOUT
IAN MCEWAN AND *ATONEMENT*

1.

Ian McEwan began his book with the image of a girl putting wild flowers in a vase, an episode that features in the second chapter of the finished novel. However, the girl – Cecilia – was originally a character in a science fiction novel, in a version of the future where the upper classes had "ditched all modern technology" and lived in "Jane Austen- style houses".

2.

On Robbie's journey to Dunkirk, he is passed by a despatch rider whose "bloodied legs dangled uselessly" (p.240), and whose pillion passenger, wounded in the arms, works the foot pedals. Ian McEwan's father was a veteran of Dunkirk; he was shot in the legs by the machine gunner of a German tank, and reached the beaches in exactly this way. He also, like Robbie, witnessed the near- lynching of an RAF clerk. McEwan senior then stayed in hospital for six months, and, like the airman in Briony's care (p.299), swore when shrapnel was removed from his thigh, and was severely ticked off by the ward sister.

3.

Ian McEwan's mother suffered from the vascular dementia, the same disease that afflicts Briony Tallis. He described her condition in his essay, 'Mother Tongue'.

4.

In 2006, McEwan was accused of "copying" the hospital sections of the book from *No Time for Romance* by Lucilla Andrews, the memoirs of a writer who had worked as a Nightingale nurse. McEwan pointed out that he always openly acknowledged his debt in the author's note at the end of the book, but rejected the charge of plagiarism. He was defended by many other writers, including Zadie Smith, Martin Amis, John Updike and Thomas Pynchon.

5.

In an interview with The Paris Review, McEwan revealed that in an earlier draft, he wrote a short fictional authorial biography for Briony, which he originally intended to include at the end of the book. It revealed that she wrote her first novel in 1948, about her wartime experiences as a nurse, had a bestseller in the 1960s which was turned into a film starring Julie Christie, and died in July 2001.

6.

The most critical review of *Atonement* published in Britain - a rare dissenting voice amid the chorus of praise - was the novelist Anita Brookner's in The Spectator. Brookner complained that the story was too often "unconvincing" and that the ending was too "lenient". She compared the novel as a whole unfavourably to McEwan's "normally thrilling examinations of various unpleasant situations".

7.

McEwan had a brief taste of notoriety in 1979, when his television play, *Solid Geometry*, was banned because of its supposed obscenity. (It featured a pickled penis in a jar.) Though categorising himself as part of the "non-totalitarian left", he was embarrassed by the invitations to talk about censorship which followed. "That was my first run-in with elements of the left who claimed we lived in a police state, which I didn't really buy."

8.

In 2008 McEwan, who grew up in Libya, attacked Islamism for its views on women and homosexuality. He said that certain streams of Christianity were "equally absurd" and that he didn't like "these medieval visions of the world according to which God is coming to save the faithful and to damn the others".

9.

McEwan was hesitant to write the screenplay for Joe Wright's 2007 film of *Atonement*, claiming it might be "a little dull." Instead, the task was given to Christopher Hampden, whose finished script was considered by actor James McAvoy (who took the role of Robbie) to be the best he'd ever read.

Ian McEwan pictured in 2012

10.

McEwan struggled for months with the Dunkirk section: he found it hard to make Robbie's drama register amid the chaos, and to tell such a well-known story from an interesting perspective. He told The New Yorker that he was hiking in Andalucia with his wife Annaleena McAfee - he is a keen walker - when it came to him: "I realized, It's a hike. I'm not going to write about the Dunkirk evacuation. I'm going to write about Robbie trying to get to the beach."

Rooms and windows play an important role in *Atonement*. Briony observes, and misinterprets, the crucial fountain scene out of the nursery window; the book ends with her looking out of the window of her hotel room over the park. Sight turns out, in the novel, to be fallible, or vulnerable to preconceptions. During her interview about Lola's rape, the inspector asks her what she saw:

> "You saw him [Robbie] then."
> "I know it was him."
> "Let's forget what you know. You're saying you saw him."
> "Yes, I saw him." (p.181)

As suggested earlier, in the section on points of view, the novel is all about perception and misperception. The room and window motifs remind us that we are each trapped inside our own individual consciousness, seeing the outside world, as the bible says, through a glass darkly.

The Tallis house was built by Cecilia's grandfather, a successful lock manufacturer – a man who "understood the value of privacy" (p.145). John Mullan suggests that "the barriers and connections between rooms shape the drama of the first half of *Atonement*, a tale of concealed passions and resentments". Think, for instance, of

Chapter Six, in which Emily lies in bed listening to the various noises from the different rooms in the house. "The country house has proved particularly hospitable to the novelist," continues Mullan. "Its interior spaces permit both secrecy and unexpected encounters. It spills out into some regulated yet possibly liberating 'outside' (where strange and dangerous things happen...)."

This brings us to the weather, which provides an important symbolic context for the novel. "I love England in a heat wave," says Leon Tallis. "It's a different country. All the rules change" (p.128). Emily Tallis remembers that her parents thought "hot weather encouraged loose morals amongst young people... Fewer layers of clothing, a thousand more places to meet. Out of doors, out of control." Mullan notes that "sometimes disastrously, heat releases the English from reserve and novelists have often used it for episodes of sexual awakening." The weather provides a countervailing force against the house, with its carefully organised, socially stratified spaces: Jack Tallis, we are told, has "precise ideas about where and when a woman should be seen smoking" (p.46).

Under pressure from the heat, things start to become unhinged, to seem out of kilter, even slightly mad. An entirely inappropriate roast dinner is served, at 10pm on a very hot night, preceded by disgusting chocolate cocktails; the children stay up far too late, and run off into the garden (out of doors, out of control). A tense, hallucinatory atmosphere is created, perhaps recalling the visual distortions of Emily's migraines, or Briony's delusions, or the "too-vivid, untrustworthy impressions" (p.98) that Cecilia has been experiencing all day.

Major themes

Guilt and atonement

The word atonement has two meanings: first, the general sense of a "reparation for a wrong or injury"; secondly, a specifically theological sense of the reconciliation of a sinful mankind to God through a sacrifice (in Christianity, through the death of Jesus). *Atonement* is the story of a crime committed by a young woman, and of her attempts to make amends for it. We learn, for instance, that Briony has passed up the chance to go to Cambridge, and seems to have "taken on nursing as a sort of penance" (p. 212). On the face of it, her main attempt to make reparation is her offer, when she visits Cecilia and Robbie, to write to her parents and correct her testimony. She doesn't expect "to be forgiven" (p.349), but she hopes to bring the matter to a happy ending, consoling herself with the thought that, when she visits them in Part Three, "their love" is still intact: "Neither

Briony nor the war had destroyed it". The section ends with the following words:

> *She knew what was required of her. Not simply a letter, but a new draft, an atonement, and she was ready to begin. (p.349)*

However, this term "a new draft" turns out to have an ambiguous meaning. In fact, in the epilogue we learn that Briony and the war, together, have indeed "destroyed" their love. So her only real form of atonement is the book that she has written. Briony suggests that this is one way of making good:

> *I like to think that it isn't weakness or evasion, but a final act of kindness, a stand against oblivion and despair, to let my lovers live and to unite them at the end. I gave them happiness, but I was not so self-serving as to let them forgive me. (p.371-2)*

But what kind of reparation is that: writing a happy ending to atone for ruining their lives? "The title of the book seems to suggest that Briony will do something by way of atonement, but nothing quite fitting this description seems to occur," argues Frank Kermode. And indeed the book admits this, in an important passage:

> *The problem these fifty-nine years has been this: how*

can a novelist achieve atonement when, with her
absolute power of deciding outcomes, she is also
God? There is no one, no entity or higher form that
she can appeal to, or be reconciled with, or that can
forgive her. There is nothing outside her. In her
imagination she has set the limits and the terms. No
atonement for God, or novelists, even if they are
atheists. It was always an impossible task, and that
was precisely the point. The attempt was all. (p.371)

In its simplest sense, this passage suggests that
there can be "no atonement": Briony can make her
stand against oblivion, can offer Cecilia and
Robbie a final kindness, but it is obviously only a
symbolic attempt. The detail of the argument,
however, is hard to follow. There is, as John
Lanchester points out, "a blurriness here":

> A novelist's responsibility to her characters is not
> at all the same thing as her responsibility to other,
> real, people. Atonement is an ethical rather than
> an aesthetic idea; it doesn't make sense to talk
> about atoning to a fictional being. Briony seems
> not to notice this – which is in character, since
> her sense of other people's existence was always
> weaker than her desire to have the world 'just so'.
> She ties things up, and leaves us feeling not quite
> at our ease...

Furthermore, Briony is not the only guilty party.

What about Paul Marshall's guilt? Or Lola's? Or the whole Tallis family's, for choosing "to believe the evidence of a silly, hysterical little girl" (p.209)? Meanwhile, the war seems to make the whole question of individual guilt seem irrelevant. Passing through a bombed French village, Robbie asks himself: "Who could ever describe this confusion, and come up with the village names and the dates for the history books? And take the reasonable view and begin to assign the blame?" (p.227). Briony may change her evidence, and "rewrite the past so that the guilty became the innocent. But what was guilt these days?" he asks, traumatised by his failure to save various people on the way to Dunkirk. "It was cheap. Everyone was guilty, and no one was... You killed no-one today. But how many did you leave to die?" (p.261). This seems to refer to the Christian sense of atonement: the idea of the wider sinfulness of mankind, requiring individual sacrifice. "Everyone had suffered," we are told as an angry mob surrounds the RAF clerk in the café, "and now someone was going to pay" (p.251).

Social class

The underlying tension that drives the action of the novel is the position of Robbie Turner in the Tallis household: as someone who associates relatively freely with the family, is at least as intelligent and has a similar education, yet is of a very different class; the child of a servant among the children of a landowner. Robbie had "spent his childhood moving freely between the bungalow and the main house"; Leon and Cecilia were his "best friends" (p.86). At Cambridge, however, Cecilia finds their relationship "awkward – That's our cleaning lady's son, she might have been whispering to her friends as she walked on" (p.79). Robbie's "childhood friend", he reflects in his bedroom, is now "in danger of becoming unreachable" (p.80).

The novel makes it clear that class is ultimately fluid. Cecilia discovers, while researching her family tree, that "on the paternal side, at least until her great-grandfather opened his humble hardware store, the ancestors were irretrievably sunk in a bog of farm labouring..." (p.21). Nevertheless, class prejudice is a powerful force. Emily Tallis regards Robbie's education as "a hobby" of her husband Jack's, "living proof of some levelling principle he had pursued through the years" (p.151). She herself sees it as "meddling", and "unfair on Leon and the girls". "'Nothing good will come of it' was the phrase she often used..." (p.152). Even Briony is very aware of the class differences, reflecting that a relationship between Robbie and Cecilia would be one that "leaps across boundaries" (p.38).

Atonement takes a fairly scathing view of the

upper class, or least parts of it. Leon, though charming, is described as living a life of "agreeable nullity" (p.109). His friend Paul Marshall, the chocolate millionaire, is gauche and self-obsessed, not to mention a rapist. Cecilia contemplates "how deliciously self-destructive it would be, almost erotic, to be married to a man so nearly handsome, so hugely rich, so unfathomably stupid" (p.50). Nevertheless, Emily is clearly well-disposed towards Marshall; and crucially, he appears to be above suspicion when Lola is raped; suspicion falls primarily on Robbie, the social experiment from which no good will come, and to a lesser extent on another member of the servant classes, Danny Hardman. "Now that I've broken away," writes Cecilia later in a letter to Robbie, "I'm beginning to understand the snobbery that lay behind their stupidity. My mother never forgave you your first... Leon turned out to be a grinning, spineless idiot who went along with everyone else" (p.209). Ironically, at this time she has also been blinded by her own prejudices: she thinks Hardman is the rapist.

The epilogue gives a glimpse of a less class-bound modern Britain. After being driven by a West Indian taxi driver who is a post-doctoral law student, Briony concludes:

> *"It's quite impossible these days to assume anything about people's educational level from the way they*

*talk or dress or from their taste in music. Safest to
treat everyone you meet as a distinguished
intellectual." (p.362)*

Nevertheless, Lord and Lady Marshall, rich and
eminent, remain untouchable when she sees them
at the Imperial War Museum.

War

"As in all McEwan's midlife work," writes
Hermione Lee, "a private drama of loss of
innocence or betrayal is played out against a larger
history of bad faith." In *Atonement*, Robbie's story
is played out against the larger history of the
Second World War. This is glimpsed proleptically
in Part One, even amid the "timeless, unchanging
calm" (p.19) of the Tallis house and park: there is
talk of Hitler, "re-armament and the Abyssinia
Question" (p.9); meanwhile, the story of Uncle
Clem and his vase reminds us of the human cost of
the First World War. In his work at the Ministry,
Jack Tallis estimates civilian casualties in their
millions from a bombing war, along with
"exchange controls, rationing, the mass evacuation
of large towns, the conscription of labour" (p.149).

In Part Three, Briony reflects that: "Her secret
torment and the public upheaval of war had always
seemed separate worlds, but now she understood
how the war might compound her crime" (p.288).

The war does indeed compound the injustices of the first section: it makes Paul Marshall rich by selling Amo bars, and it kills Robbie. Robbie explicitly draws a parallel between his own maltreatment by a snobby, complacent Establishment Britain, and the disaster that has befallen the British army in France: "A dead civilisation. First his own life ruined, then everybody else's" (p.217).

In Britain, Dunkirk is generally regarded as a heroic episode. In an interview, McEwan remarked that "tens of thousands of people died in that retreat, and yet we have a rather fond memory of it in the national narrative, and you want to play off something of the sentimentality of the 'miracle' of Dunkirk against the reality for ordinary soldiers as they made their way towards the beaches".

McEwan's version is extremely unsentimental. He avoids depicting the moment most exploited by British propaganda: the small ships rescuing the BEF from the jaws of disaster. Instead, he concentrates on the mayhem of an army in retreat. There's no glory, nor even any fighting: just soldiers running away from the enemy, looking for food and drink, being bombed, disobeying officers, turning on each other. The operation is described as a "shambles" (p.228) and later "a fucking shambles" (p.318). The beach itself provides no consolation: "there was a rout," thinks Robbie, "and this was its terminus... this was what happened when a chaotic

A scene in Joe Wright's 2007 film adaptation of Atonement

retreat could go no further." (p.247) James Wood
remarks:

> I doubt that any English writer has conveyed
> quite as powerfully the bewilderments and
> humiliations of this episode in World War II.

Dunkirk and the
British Expeditionary Force

After the outbreak of World War Two in
September 1939, a British Expeditionary Force
(p.210) commanded by Lord Gort (p.221) was sent
to help defend France against German aggression
– and was deployed largely along the Franco-
Belgian border. Fighting did not begin until 10th
May 1940, when German troops invaded France,
along with neutral Belgium and the Netherlands.
Allied forces were entirely unprepared for the
blitzkrieg – "lightning war" – unleashed on them,
spearheaded by paratroopers, tanks (see the
Panzer division on p.216) and dive-bombers (such
as the Stuka on p.236).

This is the significance of the reference to
"Liddell Hart's book" (p.288): Liddell Hart was a
veteran of World War One and a theoretician of
fast-moving, mechanised warfare. The German
army absorbed his theories and others like them,
whereas the more conservative British failed to.
The French generals, meanwhile, were still
fighting the last war: anticipating a new Western
Front, they had committed vast resources to the
heavily defended Maginot Line of forts on the

German border, which the Nazi strategy rendered irrelevant.

Hence the taunts of "Maginot!" (p.234) from the tommies (British soldiers) to the *poilus* (their French counterparts).

By May 11th, the Belgian line was broken; on May 13th the Dutch surrendered. On 15th May German forces – having advanced through the supposedly impassable Ardennes Forest – crossed the River Meuse into France at Sedan, routing French forces and allowing German tanks to pour over the border. They reached the Channel at the mouth of the River Somme on May 20th, cutting off most of the BEF and other Allied forces, which had advanced north into Belgium. Those forces then fell back in disorder on Dunkirk, the only Channel port still accessible, to await evacuation by the Royal Navy.

Crucially – for reasons that historians still argue about – on May 24th the German tanks were ordered to halt for two days. In the meantime, the British and French units protecting the BEF's rear were able to construct defences: see the Coldstream Guards holding the bridge over the canal, "silently contemptuous of the filthy disorganised rabble trailing by" (p.243). Meanwhile, the German air force, the Luftwaffe, continued to inflict heavy losses on British ships and Allied soldiers at and around Dunkirk. The Royal Air Force, though outnumbered and relatively badly-equipped, is today thought to have played a crucial role is allowing the evacuation to proceed, but the aerial battles it fought were not visible to the troops on the ground. From their point of view, the Luftwaffe had the "freedom of the skies" (p.251): hence the continual complaint of characters in *Atonement* – "Where's the RAF?" – and the attack on the blameless RAF clerk (p.251).

Between 27th May and 4th June in Operation Dynamo, a total of 330,000 British and French troops were evacuated from Dunkirk and the beaches surrounding it. After the docks were bombed, a large number of British small ships – tugboats, fishing boats, pleasure craft – crossed the Channel and helped them to embark from shallow waters. Winston Churchill hailed the rescue of the bulk of the BEF as a "miracle of deliverance" in his "We shall fight on the beaches" speech of June 4th; even today, the "Dunkirk spirit" is often invoked. However, the BEF lost 11,000 soldiers during the Battle of France, along with 14,000 wounded and 41,000 taken prisoner. It also had to leave behind a vast amount of its heavy equipment – guns, tanks, vehicles, stores and even rifles – in France.

Opposite: British soldiers wade out to a waiting destroyer off Dunkirk during Operation Dynamo

Literary tradition and storytelling

"Part of the intention of *Atonement* was to look at storytelling itself," Ian McEwan told an interviewer. "And to examine the relationship between what is imagined and what is true. It's a novel full of other writers." *Atonement* tells the story of its own composition, from Briony's moment of inspiration by the window, through its early drafts, and later modifications, to the final corrections in the Imperial War Museum. It also offers a brief history of fictional technique. It asks, Hermione Lee suggests, "what the English novel has inherited and what it can do now". "Six decades later," we are told, Briony "would describe how at the age of thirteen she had written her way through a whole history of literature, beginning with stories derived from the European tradition of folk tales, through drama with a simple moral intent, to arrive at an impartial psychological realism which she had discovered for herself, one special morning during a heatwave in 1935" (p.41).

We also learn that the early drafts of the story were explicitly modernist. Virginia Woolf complained in her essay "Modern Fiction" (1921) that her Edwardian predecessors were so concerned with the material world that they neglected psychology, so conventionally keen "to provide a plot, to provide comedy, tragedy, love interest", that they missed life's basic truths. She wanted writers instead to "record the atoms as they fall upon the mind in the order in which they fall", to "trace the pattern, however disconnected and incoherent in appearance, which each sight or incident scores upon the consciousness".

In Part Three, we learn that Briony is very impressed by Woolf's *The Waves*, and has clearly tried to imitate her work in her early draft, Two Figures by a Fountain:

> *"What excited her about her achievement was its design, the pure geometry and the defining uncertainty which reflected, she thought, a modern sensibility. The age of clear answers was over. So was the age of characters and plots... she no longer really believed in characters. They were quaint devices that belonged to the nineteenth century. The very concept of character was founded on errors that modern psychology had exposed. Plots too were like rusted machinery whose wheels would no longer turn... It was thought, perception, sensations that interested her, the conscious mind as a river through time, and how to represent its onward roll..." (p.281)*

Later on, however, Cyril Connolly's letter suggests that in her desire to concentrate on the "crystalline present moment" (p.312), Briony has thrown "the baby of fictional technique out with the folk-tale water" (p313). Readers, he argues, retain "a childlike desire to be told a story, to be held in suspense, to know what happens" (p.314). "Simply put, you need the backbone of a story." Briony's finished version has clearly been rewritten in the light of Connolly's criticisms: it retains a Woolf-style interest in consciousness and the present moment; but it also has a gripping plot, tragedy and love interest, not to mention an interest in the material world (see the section on detail). In this sense, again, it might be described as a post-modernist work. McEwan has said that he is keen to escape what he calls "the dead hand of modernism", but he also seeks to incorporate some of its techniques: "I'm always drawn to some kind of balance between a fiction that is self-reflective on its own processes, and one that has a forward impetus too, that will completely accept the given terms of the illusion of fiction." James Wood suggests that in *Atonement* he achieves "that most difficult task, the simultaneous creation of a reality that satisfies as reality while signaling itself as fiction".

Atonement examines storytelling in a moral sense, too. Briony's writerly impulses are to some extent destructive. She is "possessed" by a meddling "desire to have the world just so" (p.4), as well as by the "savage and thoughtless curiosity" (p.113) that leads her to rip open Robbie's obscene letter to Cecilia. Together with a powerful imagination that means she can't quite distinguish between what is reality and fantasy, these wreak havoc on those around her. But the novel also describes another, more humane aspect to the storytelling impulse. This is described, once again, after her epiphany at the fountain. Having tired of her play, a drama with a "simple moral intent", Briony realises:

> *There did not need to be a moral. She need only show separate minds, as alive as her own, struggling with the idea that other minds were equally alive. It wasn't only wickedness and scheming that made people unhappy, it was confusion and misunderstanding; above all, it was the failure to grasp the simple truth that other people are as real as you. (p.40)*

This conclusion finds a reflection in a well-known essay that McEwan wrote after the 9/11 attacks, which stated:

> Imagining what it is like to be someone other than yourself is at the core of our humanity. It is the essence of compassion, and it is the beginning of morality.

Atonement is both a criticism and a defence of fiction. It is, as Terry Eagleton writes, "an allegory of art and its moral contradictions... It is not hard to read this novel as McEwan's own atonement for a lucrative lifetime of magnificent professional lying."

Criticisms of *Atonement*

The most common complaint about *Atonement* concerns the ending – the surprise revelation that Robbie and Cecilia in fact died and were never reunited. "Some readers have felt cheated by it," notes John Mullan, "like viewers of *Dallas* who were suddenly shown by desperate scriptwriters that the traumatic events of many previous episodes were just Pam Ewing's 'dream'." There seem to be two aspects to this criticism. First, that it is allegedly a cheap trick. James Wood, for instance, argues that "it is unnecessary because the novel has already raised, powerfully but murmuringly, the questions that the final revelation shouts out". We know, by the end of Part Three, that Briony is the writer of the story, and that she is not altogether reliable; we know that her narrative, "a new draft, an atonement" (p.349), might thus be subject to all sorts of distortions and self-justifications.

Secondly, readers complain that the finale violates the unspoken contract between the writer and the reader. McEwan offers a conventional romantic ending, with the lovers reunited. Then he snatches it away. The move exposes and frustrates what Connolly might call one's childlike readerly desires – to be told a story with a happy ending. In the epilogue, Briony writes: "I know there's a certain kind of reader who will be compelled to ask, But what really happened?" (p.371). That reader, it is implied, is fairly unsophisticated, and at one level that must be right: obviously, this is a novel, and none of it is true. On the other hand, one could argue that since everyone knows that fiction is fiction, exploiting this fact at a crucial moment is no more interesting than saying that it was all a dream. Margaret Boerner complains: "In a kind of lunacy that one supposed he imagined was like Ionesco's absurdity, McEwan destroys the structure he has set up and tells us it was all fiction. But we knew it was all fiction."

One could argue, however, in defence of the ending, that *Atonement* is a highly self-conscious novel; that it draws attention to its own status as a piece of fiction throughout. The ending is certainly not a thematic aberration. Indeed, the novel repeatedly focuses on the role of fantasy and narrative in life; on the ability to imagine better outcomes as a crucial consolatory function. In his delirious state on the Bray Dunes, Robbie imagines being able to go back and rescue the dead boy in the tree. Similarly, it seems all too believable that someone in Briony's position might have spent years daydreaming about a less tragic outcome for Cecilia and Robbie; in this sense her rewriting of the story, her "stand against oblivion and despair" (p.371), and her revelation of the real truth, provides a moving finale. Michiko Kakutani, for instance, argues that McEwan deploys his "glittering narrative pyrotechnics" in "the service of a larger, tragic vision".

More generally, critics have sometimes criticised McEwan's for being an excessively manipulative writer. The desire to fascinate readers arguably leads him on to difficult terrain. "McEwan," complains James Wood, "is addicted to the withholding of narrative information, the hoarding of surprises, the deferral of revelations." In particular, he is addicted to the sensational turning point. The narrator of his novel *Black Dogs* expresses some scepticism about the validity of such devices:

> Turning points are the inventions of storytellers and dramatists, a necessary mechanism when a life is reduced to, traduced by a plot, when a morality must be distilled from a series of actions, when an audience must be sent home with something unforgettable to mark a character's growth. Seeing the light, the moment of truth, the turning point, surely we borrow these from Hollywood or the Bible to make retroactive sense of an overcrowded memory?

At any rate, the crucial turning point in *Atonement* is arguably somewhat contrived. No doubt the rape scene and the aftermath are masterfully designed and controlled, but the reader is entitled to ask whether such an outcome is really likely. Various reviewers have complained of "quite implausible moments" and "unlikelihoods" in the plot of *Atonement*. Would, for instance, a 13-year-old girl have been regarded as a plausible witness? Is it not probable that a sex crime in a country house in 1930s England would have been hushed up, rather than prosecuted in short order by the Surrey constabulary, because of the stigma attached to the victims of rape? The plot is, in general, perhaps overly neat. "I've always liked to make a tidy finish," writes Briony (p.353) – but is it really likely that so many of the 1935 cast should happen to reassemble on her 77th birthday: not just the family reunited at the house, but also the Marshalls, glimpsed outside the Imperial War Museum? Yet when accused of thriller-ish gimmicks, McEwan has often cited in his defence Henry James's dictum that the only obligation of a novel "is that it be interesting". And his many readers would surely agree.

Literary allusions in *Atonement*

Atonement's three main characters are writers or students of literature, and the book is studded with significant literary allusions.

Epigraph: from Jane Austen's *Northanger Abbey* (1817), in which Catherine Morland, a young woman staying with the Tilney family in the eponymous abbey, has her head turned by reading too much Gothic fiction, and entertains melodramatic fantasies about the father of the family. Austen is seen as the founding genius of the English country house novel, while the question quoted – addressed by the younger son of the Tilney family – prefigures the theme of Briony's imagination running wild: "Dearest Miss Morland, what ideas have you been admitting?"

p.4 "...the project's highest point of fulfilment." Austen's *Mansfield Park* (1814) also features a play that is rehearsed by the younger generation in the house, but never put on.

p.21 *Clarissa*. We learn that Cecilia is reading Samuel Richardson's *Clarissa* (1748). She compares Richardson unfavourably to Henry Fielding, the author of *Tom Jones* (1749). These two 18th century writers are regarded as the founders of the English novel, and are often seen to have established two separate traditions: Richardson introspective and slow-moving (Austen, James, Woolf have all been claimed as descendants); Fielding rumbustious and filled with incident (Smollett, Dickens and Thackeray continued his tradition).

p.29 The broken vase. This recalls the bowl in Henry James's *The Golden Bowl* (1904) which is thought to have a hidden flaw in it. Both the bowl and the vase are symbols of the fragility of human relationships, and both are smashed by the end of the respective novels.

p.40 "Points of view". Henry James's novels are famous for exploring point of view; McEwan has said that in writing *Atonement* he was influenced by *What Maisie Knew* (1897), the story of the daughter of irresponsible divorced parents.

p.82 Auden's Poems; Housman's *A Shropshire Lad*. See p.203 and p.262. "Mr Eliot himself" is T.S. Eliot.

p.84 Freud. Robbie's sending of the rude version of his letter is a classic example of what became known as the Freudian slip, or parapraxis: an error in speech or action which reveals a suppressed desire.

p.91 Dr Leavis: famous Cambridge critic, who named a "great tradition" of British novelists, including Jane Austen, Henry James and D.H. Lawrence, and who believed that literature had particular civilising powers.

p.128 "I love England in a heat wave. It's a different country. All the rules change." Perhaps an echo of the famous first line of L.P Hartley's *The Go-Between*: "The past is a foreign country, they do things differently there."

p.131 Malvolio: "nothing that can be can come between me and the full prospect of my desires". Malvolio is the comically frustrated lover in Shakespeare's *Twelfth Night*, a steward who becomes convinced that his mistress is in love with him; Robbie remembers playing him at college on p.82. There is a comparable social gulf between Robbie and Cecilia, the object of his desires.

p.132 *Lady Chatterley's Lover*. D.H. Lawrence's novel, which was privately printed in Italy in 1928 and not in Britain, because of its explicit descriptions of a love affair between a landowner's wife and the gamekeeper. The story, clearly, has similarities to *Atonement*'s; one of the scandalous features of Lawrence's book was the use of the word "cunt".

p.156 Briony's false rape allegation parallels that made by Adela Quested against Dr Aziz in E.M. Forster's *A Passage to India* (1924).

p.203 "In the nightmare of the dark / All the dogs of Europe bark". From the poem 'In Memory of W.B. Yeats', by W.H. Auden – a meditation on the Irish poet's passing published in 1940, and set against a backdrop of a Europe preparing for war. It contains the famous phrase "poetry makes nothing happen".

p.204 Patient Griselde: the heroine of
Chaucer's *The Clerk's Tale*, among other versions
of the same story, in which Griselde's loyalty and
obedience to her husband are subjected to a series
of awful tests, such as having her children removed
and supposedly killed. Cecilia is asked to be
patient over a number of years: "I'll wait for you,"
she tells Robbie (p.224).

p.219 Hexameter. A metrical line consisting of
six feet. An iamb is an unstresed syllable followed
by a stressed one. An anapest is two unstressed
syllables followed by a stressed one: "to the sea".

p.234-5 The descriptions of ordinary life – a
man ploughing, another teaching his son to kick a
ball – taking place "in parallel" to the war recalls
another Auden poem, 'Musée des Beaux Arts'
(1938), which begins: "About suffering they were
never wrong,/ The old Masters: how well they
understood / Its human position: how it takes
place / While someone else is eating or opening a
window or just walking dully along..."

p.242 "In the deserts of the heart / Let the
healing fountain start..." From the final stanza of
'In Memory of W.B. Yeats'.

p.262 "Oh when I was in love with you / Then I
was clean and brave." From *A Shropshire Lad*
(1896), by A.E. Housman, a cycle of poems in
which a nostalgic evocation of young men's lives in
a pastoral Shropshire ("the land of lost content") is

combined with melancholy ruminations on their early deaths, particularly in war.

p.281 Horizon was an influential British literary magazine published between 1940 and 1949.

p.309 Causse de Larzac. Features prominently in McEwan's novel *Black Dogs* (1992).

pp.312-315 C.C. is Cyril Connolly, the outstanding British critic of the period, who ran Horizon. Connolly identifies Briony's chief influence as Virginia Woolf, discussed elsewhere. Her novel *The Waves* (1931), mentioned by Briony as an inspiration (p.282), is her most experimental novel, the most concerned with fleeting mental states, the least with what Connolly here calls the "pull of simple narrative". Henri Bergson (p.314) was a French philosopher whose theories of consciousness and intuition interested Woolf and T.S.Eliot. McEwan has revealed that Elizabeth Bowen (p.314), particularly her wartime love story *The Heat of the Day* (1948), influenced the first part of *Atonement*. Another influence was Rosamond Lehmann's 1927 novel *Dusty Answer* (p.314). The novel's protagonist is brought up in a large house in Buckinghamshire, and attends Girton College, Cambridge.

p.355 "Let me not be mad." *King Lear*, Act 1 Scene 5.

p.363 Tilney's Hotel: a reference to the Tilney family, owners of Northanger Abbey.

A SHORT CHRONOLOGY

1939 1 September, World War Two breaks out

1940 The Dunkirk evacuation

1945 2 September World War Two ends

1948 21 June Ian McEwan born

1970 McEwan graduates from the University of Sussex

1976 *First Love, Last Rites*, McEwan's first short story collection, is published

1987 *The Child in Time,* which wins the Whitbread Novel Award

1998 *Amsterdam,* which wins the Booker Prize

2001 *Atonement*

2007 Joe Wright's film of *Atonement*

2010 Time Magazine names *Atonement* one of the 100 greatest novels since 1923

BIBLIOGRAPHY

Reviews and articles quoted:

Anita Brookner, "A Morbid Procedure", Spectator, 15 September 2001

Margaret Boerner, "A Bad End", Weekly Standard, 29 April 2002

Geoff Dyer, "Who's afraid of influence?", The Guardian, 22 September 2001

Terry Eagleton, "A beautiful and elusive tale", The Lancet, 22 December 2001

Frank Kermode, "Point of View", the London Review of Books, 4 October 2001

John Lanchester, "The Dangers of Innocence", The New York Review of Books, 11 April 2002

Hermione Lee, "If your memories serve you well", The Observer, 23 September 2001

Ian McEwan, "Only love and then oblivion", The Guardian, 15 September 2001

Ian McEwan, "An inspiration, yes", The Guardian, 27 November 2006

Michiko Kakutani, "And When She Was Bad She

Was...", The New York Times, 7 March 2002

John Mullan, "Guardian Book Club", The Guardian, 8-29 March 2003

James Wood, "The Trick of Truth", The New Republic, 21 March 2002

James Wood, "The Manipulations of Ian McEwan", the London Review of Books, 30 April 2009

John Updike, "Flesh on Flesh", The New Yorker, 4 March 2002

David Wiegand, "Getting rid of the ghosts", San Francisco Chronicle, March 10 2002

Daniel Zalewski, "Ian McEwan's art of unease", The New Yorker, 23 February 2009

Books quoted:

Ian McEwan, *Atonement*, Vintage, 2002; *Black Dogs*, Vintage, 1998; *Enduring Love*, Vintage, 1997

Margaret Reynolds and Jonathan Noakes, I*an McEwan: The Child in Time, Enduring Love, Atonement,* Vintage, 2002

Virginia Woolf, *The Common Reader*, Vintage Classics, 1925

First published in 2015 by
Connell Guides
Artist House
35 Little Russell Street
London WC1A 2HH

10 9 8 7 6 5 4 3 2 1

A CIP catalogue record for this book is available from the British Library.
ISBN 978-1-907776-92-2

Design © Nathan Burton
Assistant Editors and typeset by:
Paul Woodward and Holly Bruce

Printed in Malaysia

www.connellguides.com